A TREASURY *of*
MARIAN PRAYERS

A Handbook of Popular Devotions

**TWENTY-THIRD
PUBLICATIONS**
twentythirdpublications.com

Twenty-Third Publications
One Montauk Avenue, Suite 200
New London, CT 06320
(860) 437-3012 or (800) 321-0411
www.twentythirdpublications.com

Cover photo: Superstock: Rafael Jáuregui/age fotostock

ISBN: 978-1-62785-255-5
Library of Congress Catalog Card Number: 2016960020
Printed in the U.S.A.

 A division of Bayard, Inc.

CONTENTS

INTRODUCTION

Throughout the ages, we Catholics have prayed to Mary, Mother of God, as a way to express our faith, to honor the woman chosen to participate in salvation history in a unique way, and to acknowledge that since Mary is fully alive in heaven, she is, and always will be, integrally connected to us. In *Marialis Cultus*, Pope Paul VI reminds us that "Mary, in fact, is one of our race, a true daughter of Eve, though free...of sin, and truly our sister, who as a poor and humble woman fully shared our lot" (no. 56). St. John Paul II in *Redemptoris Mater* invites us to see Mary's role in today's global struggles for justice and peace. A contemporary litany of Mary calls to Mary as "Widowed mother...Seeker of God's will...Model of strength...Mother of a political prisoner."

In some Marian prayers we directly praise God because we use Mary's praise, such as in the Magnificat, or the angel's praise in the beginning of the Hail Mary. At other times Marian prayer recalls mysteries of our faith;

for example, the Angelus recalls an event in the history of God's people. This remembering also occurs during the liturgical year—for example, recalling Mary's role in the birth of Christ. Because Mary is connected with us, because she is our mother and "truly our sister," throughout our history, we have also prayed, asking Mary's intercession for our personal, communal, and world intentions.

We are privileged to know Mary as our intercessor, as well as model and witness, as one of us on this pilgrim journey. Mary is the symbol of the church, model of risk and courage, Christ-bearer to the world, advocate of those in need.

I hope that these prayers (and the many others in our Marian tradition) will provide for you a launching point for a renewed or newly discovered relationship with Mary, the woman of compassion, the faithful disciple.

Janet Schaeffler, OP

Prayers remembering Scripture events

We are gifted with many ways to pray to Mary. Because we learn about her life from Scripture and tradition, because Mary has a significant role in the mysteries of our faith, often our Marian prayer is rooted in a remembering of these cherished mysteries proclaimed in Scripture and lived throughout our tradition, reminding us of her "yes," her constant and steady fidelity.

THE ANGELUS

*In the Angelus, a meditation on Mary's "yes"
to God, we reflect on her example and ask
for her guidance and prayer.*

V. The Angel of the Lord declared unto Mary.
R. And she conceived of the Holy Spirit.
   Hail Mary...

V. Behold the handmaid of the Lord.
R. Be it done unto me according to thy word.
   Hail Mary...

V. And the Word was made Flesh.
R. And dwelt among us.
   Hail Mary...

V. Pray for us, O holy Mother of God.
R. That we may be made worthy
   of the promises of Christ.

Let us pray.
Pour forth, we beseech thee, O Lord,
    thy grace into our hearts,
    that we to whom
    the Incarnation of Christ thy Son
    was made known
    by the message of an angel,
    may by his Passion and Cross
    be brought to the glory
    of his Resurrection.
Through the same Christ Our Lord.
    Amen.

REGINA COELI

The Regina Coeli (Queen of Heaven),
an ancient Marian hymn, is prayed in place
of the Angelus during the Easter season
(Holy Saturday through the Saturday
after Pentecost).

V. Queen of Heaven, rejoice, alleluia.
R. For he whom you did merit to bear,
    alleluia.

V. Has risen, as he said, alleluia.
R. Pray for us to God, alleluia.

V. Rejoice and be glad, O Virgin Mary,
    alleluia.
R. For the Lord has truly risen, alleluia.

Let us pray.
O God,
    who gave joy to the world
    through the resurrection of your Son,
    our Lord Jesus Christ,
    grant we beseech you,
    that through the intercession
    of the Virgin Mary, his Mother,
    we may obtain the joys
    of everlasting life.
Through the same Christ our Lord.
    Amen.

THE MAGNIFICAT

*This prayer of Mary, found in Luke's gospel
(1:46–55), flows from several Old Testament
texts of praise. We pray this prayer with gratitude,
praise, and commitment to see the world through
God's eyes.*

My soul proclaims the greatness
    of the Lord,
my spirit rejoices in God my Savior
for he has looked with favor
    on his lowly servant.
From this day all generations
    will call me blessed:
the Almighty has done great things for me,
and holy is his Name.

He has mercy on those who fear him
in every generation.
He has shown the strength of his arm,
he has scattered the proud in their conceit.

He has cast down the mighty
   from their thrones,
and has lifted up the lowly.
He has filled the hungry with good things,
and the rich he has sent away empty.

He has come to the help
   of his servant Israel
for he remembered his promise of mercy,
the promise he made to our fathers,
to Abraham and his children forever.

THE ROSARY

The Rosary, named for the string of beads ("crown of roses") used to count its prayers, is a scriptural reflection on the lives of Jesus and Mary. The string is divided into sets of "decades": one Our Father, ten Hail Marys and one Glory Be in each decade. The traditional fifteen decades prayed since the sixteenth century were expanded by Saint John Paul II to include five additional reflections on the public life of Jesus. While we recite the prayers that form the backdrop of the Rosary, we meditate on the mysteries of our faith.

THE JOYFUL MYSTERIES

- The Annunciation of the Angel Gabriel to Mary
- The Visitation of Mary to Elizabeth
- The Birth of Jesus
- The Presentation of Jesus
- The Finding of Jesus in the Temple

THE LUMINOUS MYSTERIES
- The Baptism of Jesus in the Jordan River
- The Wedding at Cana
- The Proclamation of the Kingdom
- The Transfiguration of Our Lord
- The Institution of the Eucharist

SORROWFUL MYSTERIES
- The Agony of Jesus in the Garden
- The Scourging at the Pillar
- Jesus is Crowned with Thorns
- Jesus Carries the Cross
- The Crucifixion of our Lord

THE GLORIOUS MYSTERIES
- The Resurrection of Jesus Christ
- The Ascension of Jesus into Heaven
- The Descent of the Holy Spirit
- The Assumption of Mary into Heaven
- Mary is Crowned Queen of Heaven and Earth

THE ROSARY
OF THE SEVEN SORROWS

*Rather than decades, this rosary (or chaplet) con-
sists of seven sets of seven beads, each focused specifi-
cally on the seven sorrows, or dolors, of Mary (the
prophecy of Simeon, the flight into Egypt, the loss
of Jesus in the temple, Mary meeting Jesus on the
road to Calvary, the Crucifixion, Jesus being taken
down from the cross, and the laying of Jesus' body in
the tomb). Like all rosaries, this is a meditation on
the mystery-events of God's love as reflected in the
life of Jesus and Mary. It invites us to meditate on
those times in the life of Mary when she experienced
the pain and suffering that tested her faith and
invited her to a full sharing of the mystery of God's
abundant life in her son, Jesus.*

THE FRANCISCAN ROSARY

This rosary consists of seven decades, rather than five, plus two additional Hail Mary beads, for a total of seventy-two Hail Mary beads. When praying the Franciscan Rosary, the meditation focuses on the seven joys of Mary, one joy per each decade. These seven joys are the Annunciation, the Visitation of Mary to Elizabeth, the Nativity of Jesus, the Epiphany, the presentation of Jesus in the temple, the Resurrection of Jesus, and the Assumption and Coronation of Mary.

Prayers recalling Mary's various titles

We call Mary Queen of Peace, first disciple, comforter of the afflicted—and the list goes on and on. The multitudinous names and titles we have given to Mary throughout the years and in various cultures show her to be our mother, our guide and witness, our intercessor in the diverse circumstances we experience throughout the joys and challenges of our lives.

PRAYER TO OUR LADY OF GUADALUPE

When Mary appeared to the poor peasant Juan Diego in 1531 on Tepeyac Hill, Mexico, she assured us that everyone is important in God's eyes.

Dear Mother, we love you.
We thank you for your promise
    to help us in our need.
We trust in your love that dries our tears
    and comforts us.
Teach us to find our peace
    in your Son, Jesus,
      and bless us every day of our lives.
Help us to build a shrine in our hearts.
 Make it as beautiful as the one
    built for you on the Mount of Tepeyac.
A shrine full of trust, hope,
    and love of Jesus
      growing stronger each day.

Mary, you have chosen to remain with us
    by giving us your most wonderful
    and holy self-image
    on Juan Diego's cloak.
May we feel your loving presence as we look
    upon your face.
Like Juan, give us the courage
    to bring your message of hope to everyone.
You are our mother and our inspiration.
Hear our prayers and answer us.
    Amen.

AVE, MARIS STELLA

Star of the Sea (Maris Stella) is one of the oldest titles for Mary. The prayer, often used for travelers, reminds us that Mary is a sign of hope as we pray for a safe arrival at our destinations.

Hail, you Star of Ocean!
Portal of the sky,
Ever Virgin Mother,
Of the Lord most high.
O! by Gabriel's Ave,
Uttered long ago,
Eva's name reversing,
Establish peace below.
Break the captive's fetters;
Light on blindness pour;
All our ills expelling,
Every bliss implore.
Show yourself a mother;
Offer him our sighs,

Who for us Incarnate
Did not you despise.
Virgin of all virgins!
To your shelter take us;
Gentlest of the gentle!
Chaste and gentle make us.
Still as on we journey,
Help our weak endeavor,
'Til with you and Jesus
We rejoice forever.
Through the highest heaven,
To the Almighty Three,
Father, Son, and Spirit,
One same glory be. Amen.

PRAYER TO THE IMMACULATE HEART OF MARY

When we pray to Mary, with the title of the Immaculate Heart, we focus on Mary's compassionate love, asking her protection, strength, and care for all in God's family and ourselves.

O Most Blessed Mother,
    heart of love, heart of mercy,
    ever listening, caring, consoling,
    hear our prayer.
As your children, we implore
    your intercession with Jesus your Son.
Receive with understanding
    and compassion the petitions we place before
    you today, especially...
    (special intention).
We are comforted in knowing

your heart is ever open
to those who ask for your prayer.
We trust to your gentle care
and intercession,
those whom we love
and who are sick or lonely or hurting.
Help all of us, Holy Mother,
to bear our burdens in this life
until we may share eternal life
and peace with God forever.
Amen.

PRAYER TO MARY, HELP OF CHRISTIANS

This ancient title, found in the first centuries of Christianity, refers to Mary as Boeteia (the Helper). We are comforted, knowing that Mary is concerned about the needs of all in God's family.

Most holy and Immaculate Virgin,
   Help of Christians,
   we place ourselves
   under your motherly protection.
Throughout the Church's history
   you have helped Christians
   in times of trial, temptation, and danger.
Time and time again, you have proven
   to be the Refuge of sinners,
   the Hope of the hopeless,
   the Consoler of the afflicted,
   and the Comforter of the dying.
We promise to be faithful disciples
   of Jesus Christ, your Son,
   to proclaim his Good News

of God's love for all people,
and to work for peace and justice
in our world.
With faith in your intercession,
we pray for the Church,
for our family and friends,
for the poor and abandoned,
and all the dying.
Grant, O Mary, Help of Christians,
the graces of which we stand in need.
(Mention your intentions.)
May we serve Jesus
with fidelity and love until death.
Help us and our loved ones
to attain the boundless joy
of being forever with our Father
in heaven. Amen.
Mary, Help of Christians, pray for us!

PRAYER TO MARY, UNTIER OF KNOTS

When Pope Francis, then Jorge Mario Bergoglio, was studying in Germany, he was enchanted by a Bavarian painting of "Holy Mary, Our Lady Untier of Knots, and began promoting devotion to Mary under this title. We pray to Mary, Untier of Knots, about situations of chaos and times we feel "tied up" in our lives—especially the problems and struggles we face that seem to lack a solution.

Holy Mary, with all simplicity and patience you
    have given us an example on how to untangle
    the knots in our complicated lives.
By being our mother forever, you arrange
    and make clear the path
    that unites us to Our Lord.
Holy Mary, Mother of God and ours,
    with your maternal heart untie the knots
    that upset our lives.
We ask you to receive in your hands
    (mention who or your prayer request)

and deliver us from the chains
and confusions that have us restrained.
Blessed Virgin Mary, through your grace, your
intercession, and by your example, deliver
us from evil and untie the knots that keep us
from uniting with God,
so that once free of every confusion
and error, we may find him in all things, have
him in our hearts, and serve him
always in our brothers and sisters.
Mother of Good Counsel pray for us.
Amen.

TRADITIONAL BAVARIAN PRAYER

Litanies

One of the forms of prayer that has been within the Catholic tradition since the early centuries of the church is the litany. Though various litanies certainly differ in content and form, the key element of this form of prayer is found in its series of invocations or intercessions each followed by repetitions of the same response. Litanies are often used in communal prayer, but certainly can be prayed by individuals.

LITANY OF THE BLESSED VIRGIN MARY

The Litany of the Blessed Virgin Mary, also known as the Litany of Loreto, was first prayed in the sixteenth century. People continue to pray it frequently today, imploring Mary's assistance through many of her ancient titles that come from Scripture or the early Church fathers.

Lord, have mercy.
    Lord, have mercy.
Christ, have mercy.
    Christ, have mercy.
Lord, have mercy.
    Lord, have mercy.

Christ, hear us.
    Christ, hear us.
Christ, graciously hear us.
    Christ, graciously hear us.

God the Father of Heaven,

have mercy on us.
God the Son, Redeemer of the world,
	have mercy on us.
God the Holy Spirit, Holy Trinity, one God,
	have mercy on us.

Holy Mary,
	pray for us.
Holy Mother of God,
	pray for us.
Holy Virgin of virgins,
	pray for us.
Mother of Christ,
	pray for us.
Mother of the Church,
	pray for us.
Mother of divine grace,
	pray for us.
Mother most pure,
	pray for us.
Mother most chaste,
	pray for us.
Mother inviolate,
	pray for us.

Mother undefiled,
    pray for us.
Mother immaculate,
    pray for us.
Mother most amiable,
    pray for us.
Mother most admirable,
    pray for us.
Mother of good counsel,
    pray for us.
Mother of our Creator,
    pray for us.
Mother of our Savior,
    pray for us.

Virgin most prudent,
    pray for us.
Virgin most venerable,
    pray for us.
Virgin most renowned,
    pray for us.
Virgin most powerful,
    pray for us.
Virgin most merciful,

pray for us.
Virgin most faithful,
    pray for us.

Mirror of justice,
    pray for us.
Seat of wisdom,
    pray for us.
Cause of our joy,
    pray for us.
Spiritual vessel,
    pray for us.
Vessel of honor,
    pray for us.
Singular vessel of devotion,
    pray for us.
Mystical rose,
    pray for us.
Tower of David,
    pray for us.
Tower of ivory,
    pray for us.
House of gold,

pray for us.
Ark of the covenant,
    pray for us.
Gate of heaven,
    pray for us.
Morning star,
    pray for us.
Health of the sick,
    pray for us.
Refuge of sinners,
    pray for us.
Comforter of the afflicted,
    pray for us.
Help of Christians,
    pray for us.

Queen of angels,
    pray for us.
Queen of patriarchs,
    pray for us.
Queen of prophets,
    pray for us.
Queen of apostles,

pray for us.
Queen of martyrs,
  pray for us.
Queen of confessors,
  pray for us.
Queen of virgins,
  pray for us.
Queen of all saints,
  pray for us.
Queen conceived without original sin,
  pray for us.
Queen assumed into heaven,
  pray for us.
Queen of the most holy rosary,
  pray for us.
Queen of families,
  pray for us.
Queen of peace,
  pray for us.

Lamb of God, who takes away
  the sins of the world,
  spare us, O Lord.
Lamb of God, who takes away

the sins of the world,
graciously hear us, O Lord.
Lamb of God, who takes away
the sins of the world,
have mercy on us.

V. Pray for us, O holy Mother of God.
R. That we may be made worthy
of the promises of Christ.

Let us pray.
Grant, we beseech you,
O Lord God, that we, your servants,
may enjoy perpetual health
of mind and body;
and by the intercession
of the Blessed Mary, ever Virgin,
may be delivered from present sorrow,
and obtain eternal joy.
Through Christ our Lord.
Amen.

LITANY OF MARY OF NAZARETH

This contemporary litany expands the Litany of Loreto, expressing the needs and concerns of today's women and men.

Glory to you, God our Creator
Breathe into us new life, new meaning.

Glory to you, God our Savior
Lead us in the way of peace and justice.

Glory to you, healing Spirit
Transform us to empower others.

Response to the following: Be our guide.

Mary, wellspring of peace,
Model of strength,
Model of gentleness,
Model of trust,

Model of courage,
Model of patience,
Model of risk,
Model of openness,
Model of perseverance,

Response to the following: Pray for us.

Mother of the liberator,
Mother of the homeless,
Mother of the dying,
Mother of the nonviolent,
Mother of widowed mothers,
Mother of unwed mothers,
Mother of a political prisoner,
Mother of the condemned,
Mother of the executed criminal,

Response to the following: Lead us to life.

Oppressed woman,
Liberator of the oppressed,

Marginalized woman,
Comforter of the afflicted,
Cause of our joy,
Sign of contradiction,
Breaker of bondage,
Political refugee,
Seeker of sanctuary,
First disciple,
Sharer in Christ's passion,
Seeker of God's will,
Witness to Christ's resurrection,

Response to the following: Empower us.

Woman of mercy,
Woman of faith,
Woman of contemplation,
Woman of vision,
Woman of wisdom and understanding,
Woman of grace and truth,
Woman, pregnant with hope,
Woman, centered in God,

Let us pray.
Mary, Queen of Peace, we entrust our lives
    to you. Shelter us from war,
    hatred, and oppression.
    Teach us to live in peace,
    to educate ourselves for peace.
Inspire us to act justly,
    to revere all God has made.
    Root peace firmly in our hearts
    and in our world.
    Amen.

Intercessory prayer to Mary

We believe that because Mary was the Mother of Jesus, she is also our mother. As our mother and as one with all of us in the human family, in God's family, she lived the human faith journey as we do. This gift of connection enables us to pray with Mary as well as interceding with her to pray for us.

HAIL MARY

This most well-known prayer to Mary combines two lines from Scripture (Lk 1:28 and Lk 1:42) with a humble request for Mary to pray for us.

Hail Mary, full of grace
the Lord is with thee.
Blessed art thou among women
and blessed is the fruit of thy womb, Jesus.
Holy Mary, Mother of God,
pray for us sinners,
now and at the hour of our death.
    Amen.

SUB TUUM PRAESIDIUM

*This oldest known prayer to Mary was found in
a Greek papyrus, dated to around 300 AD. In a
spirit of simplicity, we pray for Mary's protection
and help.*

We turn to you for protection,
Holy Mother of God.
Listen to our prayers
and help us in our needs.
Save us from every danger,
glorious and blessed Virgin.
    Amen.

THE MEMORARE

In faith-filled prayer, we express our certainty
that Mary, as Mother of Jesus and our mother,
will always listen and respond to our needs.
The Memorare is a 16th-century version of
a much longer 15th-century prayer.

Remember,
    O most gracious Virgin Mary,
    that never was it known that anyone
    who fled to your protection,
    implored your help,
    or sought your intercession
    was left unaided.
Inspired with this confidence,
    I fly to you,
    O Virgin of virgins, my Mother;
    to you do I come;
    before you I stand,
    sinful and sorrowful.

O Mother of the Word Incarnate,
    despise not my petitions,
    but in your mercy
    hear and answer me. Amen.

MARY, HELP OF THOSE IN NEED

*Once again, expressing our confidence
that Mary continually cares, we pray for those
in need, for leaders, and for God's people.*

Holy Mary,
help those in need,
give strength to the weak,
comfort the sorrowful,
pray for God's people,
assist the clergy,
intercede for religious.
Mary, all who seek your help
experience your unfailing protection.
    Amen.

PRAYER OF
ST. JOHN XXIII

The faith and compassion of St. John XXIII are seen in this prayer of trust, this prayer of intercession for all people.

Holy Immaculate Mary,
help all who are in trouble.
Give courage to the faint-hearted,
console the sad,
heal the infirm,
pray for the people,
intercede for the clergy,
have a special care for nuns;
may all feel, all enjoy
    your kind and powerful assistance,
    all who now and always render,
    and will render,
    you honor,
    and will offer you their petitions.

Hear all our prayers, O Mother,
and grant them all.
We are all your children:
Grant the prayers of your children.
Amen forever.

THE MARIAN PRAYER OF ST. JOHN PAUL II

As the new millennium was beginning,
St. John Paul II wrote this prayer,
which asks Mary's protection for the church,
a petition for which we continually pray.

Mother of the Redeemer,
with great joy we call you blessed.
In order to carry out his plan of salvation,
   God the Father chose you
   before the creation of the world.
You believed in his love and obeyed his word.
The Son of God desired you for his Mother
   when he became man to save
   the human race.
You received him with ready obedience
   and undivided heart.
The Holy Spirit loved you as his mystical spouse
   and filled you with singular gifts.

You allowed yourself to be led
    by his hidden and powerful actions.
We entrust to you the Church, which
    acknowledges you and invokes you as Mother.
To you, Mother of our human family
    and of the nations,
        we confidently entrust the whole of humanity,
        with its hopes and fears.
Do not let it lack the light of true wisdom.
Guide its steps in the ways of peace.
Enable all to meet Christ, the Way, the Truth,
    and the Life.
Sustain us, O Virgin Mary,
    on our journey of faith
        and obtain for us the grace of eternal salvation.
O clement, O loving, O sweet Mother of God
    and our Mother, Mary!

OFFERING OF THE HEART

Knowing that Mary is a model for us, a model of generous love, we ask for her help to be a disciple like she was.

Virgin Mary, most loving Mother, please give me
    a heart like yours, firm in its attachments
        and of unshakable loyalty,
    an affectionate heart which radiates a discreet
        tenderness and which is open,
    a pure heart which lives in the flesh without
        being burdened by it,
    a generous heart, quick in forgetting its hurts
        and always ready to forgive,
    a considerate heart which hides a great deal
        of love in the smallest details, in the most
        humble service,
    a magnanimous heart which rejoices
        in others' triumphs and shares
        in their sorrows,

a heart which condemns no one,
     and does not tire of being confided to,
a heart taken up by Christ, totally given
to his infinite love.
Amen.

Prayers for specific needs

When new challenges, difficulties, and various needs arise in our lives, we often go to others, asking that they pray for us. In a very similar way, because we are one with Mary in the body of Christ, we often turn to her, our mother and the mother of the church. We ask her to pray for us just as we would ask our earthly mothers and fathers, sisters and brothers, daughters and sons, and friends (and acquaintances through social media) to pray for us.

PRAYER OF OPENNESS TO SERVE

Mary, my dearest Mother,
   give me your heart most beautiful,
   So pure, so immaculate,
   so full of love and humility,
   that I may receive Jesus as you did—
And go in haste to give him to others.
   Amen.

SAINT TERESA OF CALCUTTA

PRAYER TO OUR LADY IN TIME OF TROUBLE

Holy Virgin Mary, you are reigning in glory,
    with Jesus, your Son.
Remember us in our sadness.
Look kindly on all who are suffering
    or fighting against any difficulty.
Have pity on those who are separated
    from someone they love.
Have pity on the loneliness of our hearts.
Have pity on the weakness
    of our faith and love.
Have pity on those who are weeping,
    on those who are praying,
    on those who are fearful.
Holy Mother, please obtain for all of us hope
    and peace with justice.
    Amen.

PRAYER FOR LIVING A LIFE OF SERVICE

O Mary, Virgin of the Word
made flesh in your womb,
help us to be open to the Word of the Lord,
so that, having been welcomed
    and meditated upon,
it may grow in our hearts.

Help us to live, like you,
the beatitudes of believers
and to dedicate ourselves
with unceasing charity
to evangelizing all those who seek your Son.

Grant that we may serve every person,
becoming servants of the Word
    we have heard,
so that remaining faithful to it
we may find our happiness
in living it.
    Amen.

PRAYER TO MARY FOR A GOOD MIND

O Mary, my Mother,
I offer you my soul, my mind,
    and my heart.
Make of me God's instrument.
Give me a penetrating mind to discover,
    firm to judge,
    open to understand,
    free to serve the truth;

an honest mind in telling what it sees
    rather than what it wants to see;
a tolerant mind which does not dictate
    to other people,
but which explains what it sees clearly;
a mind infused by the light and the truth
    of your Son Jesus,
patient in faith,
while waiting for the vision of eternal life.
    Amen.

PRAYER TO OUR LADY OF THE NEW ADVENT

O Lady and Mother
of the One who was and is and is to come,
Dawn of the New Jerusalem,
we earnestly beseech you,
bring us by your intercession
so to live in love
that the Church, the body of Christ,
may stand in this world's dark
as fiery icon of the New Jerusalem.
We ask you to obtain for us this mercy
through Jesus Christ, your Son and Lord,
who lives and reigns
with the Father in the Holy Spirit,
one God forever and ever.
Amen.

FOR THOSE WHO SUFFER

Holy Virgin, in the midst of your glory, please do
not forget the sadnesses of those on earth.

Give your glance of mercy on those who
are suffering, those who struggle against
difficulties, and those who taste unceasingly
the bitter events of their lives.

Have pity on those who love one another
yet are separated.
Have pity on those whose hearts are isolated.
Have pity on the weakness of our faith.

Have pity on those whom we love.
Have pity on those who cry, those who pray,
those who are fearful.

Please give to all hope and peace.
Amen.

FR. HENRI PERREYVE *(France, 1831-1865)*

PRAYER TO
OUR LADY OF STUDIES

O Mary, Seat of Wisdom,
    so many persons of common intellect have
    made through your intercession admirable
    progress in their studies.
I hereby choose you as guardian
    and patron of my studies.
I humbly ask you to obtain for me
    the grace of the Holy Spirit,
    so that from now on
    I could understand more quickly,
    retain more readily,
    and express myself more fluently.
May the example of my life
    serve to honor you
    and your Son, Jesus.
Amen.

St. Thomas Aquinas

ON MOTHER'S DAY

Mary, on this day
   when we honor all mothers,
   we turn to you.
We thank the Lord whom you serve
   for the great gift of motherhood.
Never has it been known
   that anyone who sought
   your intercession was left unaided
   by grace.
Dear Mother, thank you for your Yes
   to the invitation of the angel
   which brought heaven to earth
   and changed human history.
   You opened yourself to God's word and the
   Word was made flesh
   and dwelt among us.

Dear mother,
   intercede for all of our mothers.

Ask your Divine Son to give them
the grace of surrendered love
so that they could join with you
in giving their own Fiat.
May they find daily strength to say yes
to the call to sacrificial love—
the very heart of the vocation
of motherhood.
May their love and witness
be a source of great inspiration
for all of us called to follow your Son.

On this Mother's Day,
Mother of the Word Incarnate,
pray for us who have recourse to you
in the Name of the Father,
the Son and the Holy Spirit.
Amen.

PRAYER FOR THOSE DESIRING PARENTHOOD

Mother of Christ,
    you were graced by God
    with the privilege of bearing
    our Divine Savior.
You experienced the joys
    and challenges of being a parent.
Your life was blessed with seeing Jesus
    grow from infancy and childhood,
    into his adult years
    of teaching and ministry.
With St. Joseph, you created a home
    for your family to love
    and share together.

Please intercede
    before the God of all life, that
    (here mention names)
    may conceive a baby
    and raise healthy children,

with whom they can share
the Lord's good gifts.

May their children honor them
and you by lives of virtue
and caring for others.
May their home be holy
and their family be blessed
with health, happiness, and abiding love.
Amen.

Hymns
to Mary

One of the forms of prayer—throughout all traditions—is song and music. Music can praise God, evoke awe, change our moods, create community, and inspire to action. St. Augustine, an early Church father, said, "To sing is to pray twice." Throughout the centuries, prayer to Mary has often been more than words; it has often taken the form of hymns and antiphons. Often they are sung in devotional prayer during the months of May and October, months dedicated to honoring Mary in a special way.

IMMACULATE MARY

Immaculate Mary, your praises we sing,
Who reigns now in splendor with Jesus, Our
   King.
Ave, ave, ave, Maria! Ave, ave, Maria!

In heaven the blessed your glory proclaim;
On earth, we, your children,
   invoke your sweet name!
Ave, ave, ave, Maria! Ave, ave, Maria!

We pray for our mother, the Church upon earth;
And bless, dearest Lady, the land of our birth.
Ave, ave, ave, Maria! Ave, ave, Maria!

HAIL HOLY QUEEN

Hail, Holy Queen enthroned above,
  O Maria.
Hail, mother of mercy and of love,
  O Maria.

Triumph, all ye cherubim,
  Sing with us, ye seraphim,
Heaven and earth resound the hymn:
Salve, salve, salve Regina!

Our life, our sweetness, here below,
  O Maria!
Our hope in sorrow and in woe,
  O Maria!

Triumph, all ye cherubim,
  Sing with us, ye seraphim,
Heaven and earth resound the hymn:
Salve, salve, salve Regina!

Turn then most gracious Advocate,
  O Maria!
Toward us thine eyes compassionate,
  O Maria!

Triumph, all ye cherubim,
  Sing with us, ye seraphim,
Heaven and earth resound the hymn:
Salve, salve, salve Regina!

MARY THE DAWN,
CHRIST THE PERFECT DAY

Mary the Dawn,
    Christ the Perfect Day;
Mary the Gate,
    Christ the Heav'nly Way!
Mary the Root,
    Christ the Mystic Vine;
Mary the Grape,
    Christ the Sacred Wine!
Mary the Wheat-sheaf,
    Christ the Living Bread;
Mary the Rose-Tree,
    Christ the Rose Blood-red!
Mary the Font,
    Christ the Cleansing Flood;
Mary the Chalice,
    Christ the Saving Blood!
Mary the Temple,
    Christ the Temple's Lord;
Mary the Shrine,
    Christ the God adored!

Mary the Beacon,
    Christ the Haven's Rest;
Mary the Mirror,
    Christ the Vision Blest!
Mary the Mother,
    Christ the Mother's Son.
Both ever blest while endless ages run.
Amen.

ON THIS DAY,
O BEAUTIFUL MOTHER

On this day, O beautiful Mother,
On this day we give thee our love.
Near thee, Madonna, fondly we hover,
Trusting thy gentle care to prove.

On this day we ask to share,
Dearest Mother, thy sweet care;
Aid us ere our feet astray
Wander from thy guiding way.

On this day, O beautiful Mother,
On this day we give thee our love.
Near thee, Madonna, fondly we hover,
Trusting thy gentle care to prove.

Rose of Sharon, Lovely flow'r,
Beauteous bud of Eden's bow'r;
Cherished lily of the vale,
Virgin Mother, Queen we hail.

DAILY DAILY SING TO MARY

Daily, daily sing to Mary,
Sing, my soul, her praises due.
All her feasts, her actions worship
With the heart's devotion true.
Lost in wond'ring contemplation,
Be her Majesty confess'd.
Call her Mother, call her Virgin,
Happy Mother, Virgin blest.

She is mighty to deliver.
Call her, trust her lovingly.
When the tempest rages round thee,
She will calm the troubled sea.
Gifts of heaven she has given,
Noble Lady, to our race.
She, the Queen, who decks her subjects
With the light of God's own grace.

Sing, my tongue, the Virgin's trophies
Who for us her Maker bore.
For the curse of old inflicted,
Peace and blessing to restore.
Sing in songs of peace unending,
Sing the world's majestic Queen.
Weary not nor faint in telling.
All the gifts she gives to us.

STABAT MATER

At the cross her station keeping,
Stood the mournful Mother weeping,
Close to Jesus to the last.

Through her heart, his sorrow sharing,
All his bitter anguish bearing,
Now at length the sword had pass'd.

Oh, how sad and sore distress'd
Was that Mother highly blest
Of the sole-begotten One!

Christ above in torment hangs;
She beneath beholds the pangs
Of her dying glorious Son.

Is there one who would not weep,
Whelm'd in miseries so deep
Christ's dear Mother to behold?

Can the human heart refrain
From partaking in her pain,
In that Mother's pain untold?

Bruis'd, derided, curs'd, defil'd,
She beheld her tender child
All with bloody scourges rent.

For the sins of his own nation,
Saw him hang in desolation,
Till his spirit forth he sent.

O thou Mother! fount of love!
Touch my spirit from above;
Make my heart with thine accord.

Make me feel as thou hast felt;
Make my soul to glow and melt
With the love of Christ our Lord.

Holy Mother! pierce me through;
In my heart each wound renew
Of my Savior crucified.

Let me share with thee his pain,
Who for all my sins was slain,
Who for me in torments died.

Let me mingle tears with thee,
Mourning him who mourn'd for me,
All the days that I may live.

By the cross with thee to stay,
There with thee to weep and pray,
Is all I ask of thee to give.

Virgin of all virgins best,
Listen to my fond request
Let me share thy grief divine.

Let me, to my latest breath,
In my body bear the death
Of that dying Son of thine.

Christ, when thou shalt call me hence,
Be thy Mother my defense,
Be thy cross my victory.
While my body here decays,
May my soul thy goodness praise,
Safe in Paradise with thee.
Amen.

ACKNOWLEDGMENTS

Prayer to Mary for a Good Mind
Offering of the Heart
For Those Who Suffer
Prayer to Our Lady of Studies
Translated and adapted from Fernand Lelotte, SJ, *Rabboni, Consignes et prières pour mieux servir* (Paris, Casterman, 1958), by Dr. Chau Thien Phan, Professor Emeritus, Rider University, Lawrenceville, New Jersey, and now Associate Diocesan Ecumenical Officer, Diocese of St. Augustine, Florida.

Prayer to Our Lady of the New Advent
Prayer composed by the Benedictine Nuns of the Abbey of St. Walburga, Boulder, Colorado.

Litany of Mary of Nazareth
from *The Fire of Peace: A Prayer Book*. Compiled and edited by Mary Lou Kownacki, OSB. Used with permission. www.paxchristiusa.org.

Prayer for those Desiring Parenthood
Used with permission, Oblate Missions, San Antonio, Texas.